The Phoenix Living Poets

RINGS ON A TREE

The Phoenix Living Poets

★

RINGS
ON A TREE

by

Norman MacCaig

CHATTO AND WINDUS

THE HOGARTH PRESS

1968

Published by
Chatto and Windus Ltd
with The Hogarth Press Ltd
42 William IV Street
London WC2
*
Clarke, Irwin and Co Ltd
Toronto

PR
6025
A 1628
R5

SBN 7012 0304 8

Printed in Great Britain by
William Lewis (Printers) Limited
Cardiff

Contents

Orgy

Thinking of painters, musicians, poets
who visited the world outside them and the world
inside them and brought back
their sweet discoveries, only to be devoured
by those they brought them to,
I remembered
a wood near Queensferry, where
a banquet of honeydew, that sweet exudation,
was spread on a million airy leaf-tables
in an avenue of lime trees.

Under the tables,
on the broad path below,
a million bees crawled and fell about,
blind drunk.

And a million ants
bit into their soft bellies
for the intoxicating liquor stored
in these tiny tuns — having discovered
that the innkeeper was the inn.

Rhu Mor

Gannets fall like the heads of tridents,
bombarding the green silk water
off Rhu Mor. A salt seabeast of a timber
pushes its long snout
up on the sand, where a seal,
struggling in the straitwaistcoat of its own skin,
violently shuffles towards the frayed wave,
the spinning sandgrains, the
caves of green.

I sit in the dunes — the wind
has moulded the sand in pastry frills
and cornices: flights of grass
are stuck in it — their smooth shafts shiver
with trickling drops of light.

Space opens and from the heart of the matter
sheds a descending grace that makes,
for a moment, that naked thing, being,
a thing to understand.

I look out from it
at the grave and simple elements
gathered round a barrage of gannets
whose detonations
explode the green into white.

I sit with my back to the engine, watching
the landscape pouring away out of my eyes.
I think I know where I'm going and have
some choice in the matter.

I think, too, that this was a country
of bog-trotters, moss-troopers,
fired ricks and rooftrees in the black night – glinting
on tossed horns and red blades.
I think of lives
bubbling into the harsh grass.

What difference now?
I sit with my back to the future, watching
time pouring away into the past. I sit, being helplessly
lugged backwards
through the Debatable Lands of history, listening
to the execrations, the scattered cries, the
falling of rooftrees
in the lamentable dark.

Balances

Because I see the world poisoned
by cant and brutal self-seeking,
must I be silent about
the useless waterlily, the dunnock's nest
in the hedgeback?

Because I am fifty-six years old
must I love, if I love at all,
only ideas — not people, but only
the idea of people?

Because there is work to do, to steady
a world jarred off balance,
must a man meet only a fellow-worker
and never a man?

There are more meanings than those
in text books of economics
and a part of the worst slum
is the moon rising over it
and eyes weeping and
mouths laughing.

Starlings

Can you keep it so,
cool tree, making a blue cage
for an obstreperous population? —
for a congregation of mediaeval scholars
quarrelling in several languages? —
for busybodies marketing
in the bazaar of green leaves? —
for clockwork fossils that can't be still even
when the Spring runs down?

No tree, no blue cage can contain
that restlessness. They whirr off
and sow themselves in a scattered handful
on the grass — and are
bustling monks
tilling their green precincts.

Learning

Through these streets bright as hosannahs
I see Blake walking, listening through hosannahs
to notes of woe, to the shrieks and curses
my ear is deaf to.

In these crowds of people I see Hieronymus Bosch
skinning faces, undressing she-devils, observing
mouths choked with abortions — and to all of it
my eyes are blind.

In these crowds of people I see Brueghel making
marvellous matter-of-fact notations of
unemphatic marvels — that woman, child, horse:
I see them too.

And through these streets walks Bach, giving order
to all hosannahs and adding to them, announcing
the tragedy of praise, the enrichments of grief — things
my ears are tuned to.

I walk, I see, I listen: enlarged a little
by deafness and hearing, seeing and blindness,
I begin to understand, I begin to reject
the bad lie of loneliness.

Satisfaction

In the end the fox gets the grapes
and discovers
that they are sour.

In the end
the dog runs off with the reflection
of the bone in his mouth.

I lean down like Tantalus
to drink you. Flow away, girl, your kindness
terrifies me — can't you see
it's my thirst
I am thirsty for?

Ivory Turret

Outside my window
buds are breaking.
It's that time of the year.

I listen to Wanda Landowska
making tawny sounds
on the harpsichord.

Outside my window
hearts are breaking. — Not all of them
but
hearts are breaking.
It's that time of year,
as it always is.

Inside, I listen
to buds breaking, hearts
breaking, in the lucid
timelessness
of Scarlatti.

Say this to the breaking heart,
say this to Wanda Landowska —
you'll get two answers that make
one discord.

Country Postman

Before he was drowned,
his drunk body bumping down the shallows
of the Ogle Burn, he had walked
fifteen miles every day
bringing celebrations and disasters
and what lies between them
to MacLarens and MacGregors
and MacKenzies.

Now he has no news to bring
of celebrations or disasters,
although, after one short journey,
he has reached
all the clans in the world.

In Peacetime

The thorntree on the bare moor —
beard, arms, tattered rags
stream East in ancient gestures
of execration and despair.

And yet the sun is shining, grasshoppers
spray in a bow wave from my feet,
bees bumble
over windless flowers.

The tree is a notation
of past storms; it is
a refugee
from forgotten wars.

It can't change now —
it can't spread abroad
its crippled limbs
to receive the sun,
the sun that has come
too late.

A Difference

Trying to recall
the feel of pebbles underfoot
on the beach at Kirkaig, I
recall it. But my feet
are not hurt.

Or, remembering the well
at the Bay of the Lambs and its water
exploring
the length of my throat,
I remember it, but
remain thirsty.

Memory keeps from me
that trivial hurt, this
trivial pleasure.

What it does is not
trivial, when I
remember you —
my sore journey, my draught
of pure being.

Achmelvich Well

The way the water languished
in that burning summer was
sore to see.

The two taps by the side of the road
that had staled like stallions
drooled, then sputtered, and
suffered from airlocks.

When the lid of the well was lifted
a new smell climbed out
of water that had died by hanging
on the cold walls.

At last the shrunk air
swelled and talked rain
for two days. — The well
was well again and
the taps gushed chains,
then ropes
of cloudy water.

Foiled Shepherd

I drive my little flock of beliefs
along a narrow road. They behave well
until we pass your house.

You are that parrot in Lairg
that had learned the language
whistled by shepherds. When
the Lamb Sales were on — what
confusion in the road! — what scattering,
what barking, what human execrations!

You parrot my language.
All you need now is to learn
its meaning. Then I, with my dogs
at heel, will saunter at ease
behind that flock, my mind
filled with their baaing, my face
grinning in their dust.

Antique Shop Window

Spearsman of molasses, shepherdess
cut from a sugarblock, rings with
varicose stones — all
on a one-legged table perched
on a birdclaw.

And your face in the glass and
my face in the glass, and the real world
behind us translated before us
into dim images, there
— so that the spearsman crouches
on a bird-legged table in
a busy street and the shepherdess runs
through head after head after head
and who can tell
if your face is haunted by the world
or the world by your face?

Look left at the birds stitched
still in their singing, at the sword
half drawn from the scabbard — look left,
more left, to me, this side of the window,
a two-legged, man-legged cabinet
of antique feelings, all of them
genuine.

Visiting Hour

The hospital smell
combs my nostrils
as they go bobbing along
green and yellow corridors.

What seems a corpse
is trundled into a lift and vanishes
heavenward.

I will not feel, I will not
feel, until
I have to.

Nurses walk lightly, swiftly,
here and up and down and there,
their slender waists miraculously
carrying their burden
of so much pain, so
many deaths, their eyes
still clear after
so many farewells.

Ward 7. She lies
in a white cave of forgetfulness.
A withered hand
trembles on its stalk. Eyes move
behind eyelids too heavy
to raise. Into an arm wasted
of colour a glass fang is fixed,
not guzzling but giving.
And between her and me
distance shrinks till there is none left
but the distance of pain that neither she nor I
can cross.

She smiles a little at this
black figure in her white cave
who clumsily rises
in the round swimming waves of a bell
and dizzily goes off, growing fainter,
not smaller, leaving behind only
books that will not be read
and fruitless fruits.

Signs, not Omens

I gaze at you so hard
I alter you by gazing, I alter me by gazing.

Surely others see evidence
of this in you, of this in me?

I feel like the Inverkirkaig man
who had pointed with pride so often
to the Barrel Buttress on Suilven
one looked to see his fingerprint on it —
or a sandstone fingerstall
on his finger.

— Except that I am not he, and
what, good heavens, could be more unlike you
than a Barrel Buttress?

Space Travel

I lay like someone in a ballad
under a whinbush.
A petal the size of a goblin's helmet
in a child's book
dangled so near my eye
it seemed I could be the first man
to land on it.

In a way that crumpled my face
I drew back my head to have
a clearer look, and did, and saw
creeping out of the golden helmet a red,
a malevolent, a Martian spider.

Before I came to earth
I heard something in my mind laugh
with the homicidal hilarity
of a laugh in a ballad.

Writers' Conference, Long Island University

The moderator's spectacles twinkle in the light.
His brain twinkles in five languages.
Two speakers sit on each side of him, desperately
at ease. The microphone
sucks his words in and sprays them
out again over the dry
audience. All round and overhead, glitters
a poor man's Sistine Chapel
of gold scrolls and foiled trumpets, of
pumped-up Cupids and Muses, their blank eyes
unable to show
the astonishment they're unable to feel
at the languages of the world
crackling and sibilating around them
instead of
what they were used to — the revolving orbs
of Eddie Cantor, Ethel Merman's Guinness and
velvet voice — hoofers and clowns and galvanised
tap-dancers — all gone, all gone,
now fat in penthouses or mad
in flophouses or
silent at last under the sibilating
language of grass.

The panel, tails feathering, give tongue after
an elusive quarry. But
no votes will be taken. No
resolution will be made. — That
will be left to the grass
that counts no votes but by which
a resolution will be passed that

25

no-one will contradict
in any language.

But the quarry will not
stop running. And the sweet vocables
will carry their human thoughts in pursuit of it
into territories where,
though the quarry always escapes,
new thoughts will meet them and new worlds
seem possible.

Hotel Room, 12th Floor

This morning I watched from here
a helicopter skirting like a damaged insect
the Empire State Building, that
jumbo size dentist's drill, and landing
on the roof of the PanAm skyscraper.
But now midnight has come in
from foreign places. Its uncivilised darkness
is shot at by a million lit windows, all
ups and acrosses.

But midnight is not
so easily defeated. I lie in bed, between
a radio and a television set, and hear
the wildest of warwhoops continually ululating
                              through
the glittering canyons and gulches –
police cars and ambulances racing
to the broken bones, the harsh screaming
from coldwater flats, the blood
glazed on sidewalks.

The frontier is never
somewhere else. And no stockades
can keep the midnight out.

Tugboat Poet

He calls in the dark, under
his Brooklyn Bridge of constellations,
stubbornly pushing against
the filthy tide his
useful cargo.

His crying wails through
any East Side, so sad it is
beautiful, so beautiful it is
sad.

And minds, wakeful in
midnight apartments, listen
and think of
marvellous journeys.

Brooklyn Cop

Built like a gorilla but less timid,
thick-fleshed, steak-coloured, with two
hieroglyphs in his face that mean
trouble, he walks the sidewalk and the
thin tissue over violence. This morning,
when he said, "See you, babe" to his wife,
he hoped it, he truly hoped it.
He is a gorilla
to whom "Hiya, honey" is no cliché.

Should the tissue tear, should he plunge through
into violence, what clubbings, what
gunshots between Phoebe's
Whamburger and Louie's Place.

Who would be him, gorilla with a nightstick,
whose home is a place
he might, this time, never get back to?

And who would be who have to be
his victims?

I sit on a hard seat and do not raise
my carton of weak beer to the green
Statue of Liberty whose back is turned
on Manhattan.

Negroes and whites, enfilading her
with cameras, will take her home
in proper reduction.

The guide, hobnobbing with gossip,
information, blue jokes and Readers
Digest philosophy, keeps disappearing and
returning, slightly pinker, slightly
bluer.

He points to the apartments
of the La-di-dah, the playparks of
regular kids, the UN building and
the Hospital for the Insane. But nothing is
more shot alive by a broadside of
cameras than Frank
Sinatra's penthouse.

We reduce speed for Harlem River—
like troops closing ranks
where an ambush is possible —
then turn south down the Hudson, by
the Jersey Palisades, gawping at
the "Queen Elizabeth", that tiny boat moored
to a skyscraper, and ignoring
the Statue of Liberty. We've seen her
already. We've had her.

The Sun Comes to Earth in the Bowery

The sun turns into
one, a topple of roof-copings: two,
a ripple of slatted windowblinds: three, a gangling
rapid of fire-escapes: four, a dust-fall
of scalloped steps: five, a man.

The man lies on his side. A yellow string
joins his vomit to the hole that was
his mouth. One extinguished eye
is open. One shoe has fallen off
one naked ankle. Beside him is
a paper bag from which has burst
unrecognisable rags and the hairy
bottom joint of a calf's leg.

A news-sheet tumbles in the wind,
filled with dead events: news
no longer.

Battery Park

On Sundays there is nobody on Wall Street.
This Trust and that Trust and the next
Trust stand with their heads in the clouds,
like Aztec temples and
for more than one reason. The gold-worshippers,
the dollar-men have chinked off home and
the temples are deserted
in the flowerless jungle of Manhattan.

I walk downtown through Wall Street
till the glass cliffs are stopped by the sea
and a brackish smell creeps through
the harsh stink of burnt petrol.
In the pleasant arc of the Battery, citizens
stroll, sit, eat sandwiches
and stare across
the filthy water they crept out of
millions of years ago, now chopped
by the Staten Island ferry.
Their feelings are not filial.
Old seamen stare across water
at their own history. But they
stare at a history they have
never had and cannot
reconstruct — where Nature
had something to do with the colour
green and the sound
of clear water; where Nature
tired muscles, not nerves; and was a wilderness —
but one where it was not so easy
to lose your way.

I watch the gulls
behaving as gulls do in
China or Britain —
before me, the outraged sea and behind me
the wilderness, whose temples
are deserted, their worshippers
gone off to worship their other god,
the Eternal Surrogate, whose
Sunday it is and who can be seen,
in glimpses, walking on the water
and eating sandwiches in the pleasant
arc of the Battery.

Leaving the Metropolitan Museum

I went out from the unsheltered world of art
into the unsheltered world,
and there, by the door —
Picasso's Goat —

a shape of iron entered into by herds,
by every aspect of goatishness.
(What are you to say of a man
who can carve a smell, who
can make a goat-smell out of iron?)

This is the lie of art
telling its great truth:
a shape of iron, destructible and
created, being a revelation about life,
that is destructive and
indestructible.

From now on,
whatever of life passes
my understanding, I know more of it
than I did, being
a professor of goats, a pedant
of goatishness.

A fortnight is long enough
to live on a roller-coaster.
Princes Street, Edinburgh, even in the most rushed
of rush hours, you will be
a glade in a wood, I'll wrap myself
in your cool rusticity, I'll
foretell the weather, I'll be
a hick in the sticks.

The sun goes up on Edinburgh.
Manhattan goes up on the sun.
Her buildings overtop Arthur's Seat
and are out of date as soon as
a newspaper. Last year's artist is
a caveman. Tomorrow's best seller
has still to be born.

I plunge through constellations
and basements. My brain spins up there,
I pass it on its way down. I can't see
for the skyscraper in my eye, there's a traffic jam
in my ears. My hands are tacky
with steering my bolting self
through unlikelihoods and impossibilites.
Flags and circuses orbit
my head, I am haloed but not saintly —
poor Faust in 42nd Street.
The tugs in the East River butt
rafts of freight trucks through
my veins. I look at my watch
and its face is Times Square
glittering and crawling with invitations.

Two weeks on a roller-coaster
is long enough. I remember
all islands are not called Coney.
I think, Tomorrow my head will be
higher than my feet, my brain
will come home, I'll be able
to catch up on myself — and, tilting my halo,
I walk out into
exploding precincts and street-bursts.

Truth for Comfort

So much effect, and yet so much a cause —
Where things crowd close she is a space to be in:
And makes a marvel where a nowhere was.

Now she's not here I make this nowhere one
That's her effect and it becomes a marvel
To be made marvellous when her journey's done.

Ideas can perch on a nerve and sing.
I listen to their singing and discover
That she can share herself with everything.

This chair, this jug, this picture speak as her,
If in a muted way. Is that so crazy?
My singing mind says No, and I concur.

And is this lies for comfort? She won't know
(Who could not be the cause of lies), for comfort's
What I won't need, until she has to go.

Fog at Dusk

Fogs move in drifts and where the drifting comes
Their cold webs change clear bushes into slums
Where branches blacken with an evil stain
From drops that could not ever have been rain.

The fog webs fatten the spiders' till they sag
As thick as cloths. I touch one — its cold rag
Becomes a filthy glove. Trees disappear
And come again, translating there to here.

A drift goes by. I walk out of the murk
And see, high overhead, the moon at work
Like Cinderella, though soon to be so proud,
In the cold kitchen of a sluttish cloud.

Hollows are cups of vapour. One, too full,
Spills over, slow as lava. The seapool
Is ghosted with false sails. A window's spark
Is a red eye that burns sore in the dark.

Threshing

The corn stack dwindles in
The wintry air. Jess,
The terrier, has killed twenty
Rats and looks for more . . .
He heaps chaff in a hill;
His eyes are red and sore.

They see him as he was
Twenty years ago,
Ruddy and tall and glowing,
Filled with his natural Spring —
Full of grace as a cornstalk,
His fat seed ripening.

Time clanks and smokes in the thin
And wintry air. He sees
The stack fall in and easy
Straws lying all about
While chaff heaps up in a hill
And hidden rats run out.

Fire Water

The water was still, dead black.
In it comets shot off
From the drifting boat, their track
Ten yards of greenish fire.

Corks bobbed. Arms plunged in
And were arms of fire. They plunged
Through the black water-skin
To a boiling cloud of fire.

From the fiery cloud they plucked
A salmon, cold as a saint.
Clout him. Stuff him in the rucked
Neck of the slimy sack.

Two fires quenched . . . The boat
Crept off, with a string of fire
Trailed thinly round its throat
And comets under its keel.

Winter

Shepherds, tramping the frozen bogland
Beside the sheeted ghost of Quinag,
Hear guns go off in the shrivelling air —
Not guns, ice on the frozen lochans
Whose own weight is too gross to bear.

Crofter, coughing in the morning,
Sees the pale window crossed with branches
Of a new tree. He wipes a rag
Across the glass and, there, a beggar
In his own tatters, a royal stag.

Six black stumps on the naked skerry
Draw the boat close in. The oarsman,
Feeling a new cold in his bones,
Sees cormorants, glazed to the sea-rock,
Carved out of life, their own tombstones.

Solitary Crow

Why solitary crow? He in his feathers
Is a whole world of crow — of a dry-stick nest,
Of windy distances where to be crow is best,
Of tough-guy clowning and of black things done
To a sprawled lamb whose blood beads in the sun.

Sardonic anarchist. Where he goes he carries,
Since there's no centre, what a centre is,
And that is crow, the ragged self that's his.
Smudged on a cloud, he jeers at the world then halts
To jeer at himself and turns two somersaults.

He ambles through the air, flops down and seesaws
On a blunt fencepost, hiccups and says Caw.
The sun glints greasy on his working craw
And adds a silver spot to that round eye
Whose black light bends and cocks the world awry.

The Red Well, Harris

The Red Well has gone.
Thirty years ago I filled pails from it
with a flashing dipper and floated
a frond of bracken in each
so that no splash of water should escape
from its jolting prison.

Where that eye of water once
blinked from the ground
now stands a gray house
filled with voices.

The house is solid. But
nothing will keep the children
in its happy prison
from scattering abroad, till
the house at last stands empty —
one drained well
on top of another.

Aunt Julia

Aunt Julia spoke Gaelic
very loud and very fast.
I could not answer her —
I could not understand her.

She wore men's boots
when she wore any.
— I can see her strong foot,
stained with peat,
paddling the treadle of the spinningwheel
while her right hand drew yarn
marvellously out of the air.

Hers was the only house
where I lay at night
in the absolute darkness
of the box bed, listening to
crickets being friendly.

She was buckets
and water flouncing into them.
She was winds pouring wetly
round house-ends.
She was brown eggs, black skirts
and a keeper of threepennybits
in a teapot.

Aunt Julia spoke Gaelic
very loud and very fast.
By the time I had learned
a little, she lay
silenced in the absolute black
of a sandy grave

at Luskentyre.
But I hear her still, welcoming me
with a seagull's voice
across a hundred yards
of peatscrapes and lazybeds
and getting angry, getting angry
with so many questions
unanswered.

Uncle Seumas

Mad on his small island
he scribbled by lamplight, fluttering down
great snowflakes of paper
on to the drift at his feet.

Fishermen dug his potato patch,
fetched stores from the pier, hung
on his door handle
small bombs of fish.

Behind barricades and shutters
he listened to them, his eyes
sore with terror. They prowled
in the darkness of his mind.

When men came and took him away,
mad king of his small island,
he left behind him his people
buried, dead, in the paperdrifts.

Now and For Ever

I watch seven sails going in seven directions —
but all heeled over one way.
This satisfies
the dying Calvinist in me,
who is corrupt enough, anyway,
to observe that, if you can't escape
the wrath of God, you can't escape His pleasure
either.

(I remember this morning,
when a marmalade cat made a small rainbow of itself
whose crock of gold was
a rabbit in a bracken bush.
I walked away
from the thin screaming, I couldn't stand
the decorum of that death.)

I dribble through my fingers
what was a rock once
and in my little doomsday
look with unreturned love at a cloud,
at the sea, at a rock where
a cormorant, wings half spread, stands
like a man proving to his tailor
how badly his suit fits.

Sleeping Compartment

I don't like this, being carried sideways
through the night. I feel wrong and helpless — like
a timber broadside in a fast stream.

Such a way of moving may suit
that odd snake the sidewinder
in Arizona: but not me in Perthshire.

I feel at rightangles to everything,
a crossgrain in existence. — It scrapes
the top of my head, my footsoles.

To forget outside is no help either —
then I become a blockage
in the long gut of the train.

I try to think I am a through-the-looking-glass
mountaineer bivouacked
on a ledge five feet high.

It's no good. I go sidelong.
I rock sideways . . . I draw in my feet
to let Aviemore pass.

Old Man Thinking

Oars, held still, drop
on black water
tiny roulades
of waterdrops.
With their little sprinkling
they people
a big silence.

You who are long gone,
my thoughts of you are like that:
a delicate, clear population
in the big silence
where I rest on the oars and
my boat
hushes ashore.

Estuary

Saltings and eelgrass
and mud dimpling under the moon —
a place for curlews but not for me; a place
for dunlin, godwit, sandpiper, turnstone
but not for me.

The light is blue. The far away tide
shines like a fish in a cupboard.

I see the blues of your eyes.

Don't step on the little green crab.
Don't step on the mud hump, it will hold you
in a soft fist.

Your brow shines. The inside
of a mussel shell shines. I make
horrible correspondences.

Somewhere behind us
a clear river has died, its muscles
gone slack, its innumerable voices turned
into sounds of sucking and slithering.

Can we turn back? Let me take
your hand, cold as eelgrass, and look for
a meadow furred with fresh water, let me
turn the blues of your eyes away
from the moon dimpling in mud.

By correspondence then
your eyes will be clear, you will
sometimes look at me, you will laugh
at the lolloping hare or the hedgehog trundling by

like a mediaeval siege engine — at a world
of beginnings, at a world of possibly
desperate ends, but
a world of beginnings.

Small Round Loch

Lochan Dubh is too small
for any wind to lash it
into the vulgarity of crashing waves
and spit spray. In any storm
it finnicks amongst its reeds and pebbles
with inextinguishable preciosity —
a watchmaker of light and water,
making itself.
I see a jewel here, a jewel there,
small emerald, chip of diamond, minuscule
sapphire, taking the strain
of light
swivelling on water:
delicate mechanism, measuring
a time
that has no escapement.

Illumination: On the Track by Loch Fewin

Suddenly the sun poured
through an arrow-slit in the clouds
and the great hall we walked in — its tapestries
of mountains and parquet of rich
bogland and water — blazed on the eye
like the Book of Kells.

For four days a cloud
had sat like a lid on the round
horizon. But now
we walked in a mediaeval manuscript —
doves flew over the thorn, the serpent
of wisdom whispered
in our skulls and our hands
were transparent with love.

A Sort of Blues

Look at me — failed St.Sebastian, vainly
summoning the arrows
that stand on their heads
in quivers everywhere.

— What have I done
to deserve this sort of peace?
I see suffering all around me.
What have I done that I
should be exempt from it?

Don't I sin too? Am I not
as proper a victim as anyone
for misfortune and injustice?

To be ignored is the worst.
— My luck to live in a time
when to be happy
is to have no neighbours.

Names and their Things

You stood by a window in Amherst
pointing to names I knew
that became birds.
I stood with you
watching a familiar word
turn into a hickory tree.

So many names in my mind
are naked of their meanings —
scrod, Popocatapetl, rickshaw —
even freedom, even justice: but not
love, nor, any more,
grackle and chickadee
that flew into my mind
that summer morning
and perched there beside
a mourning dove.

New England Theocritus

They boil it and boil it till
a thimbleful, neat, is
enough to swallow.

This is all right for maple syrup,
but not for me, not for you.

I will not reduce and concentrate
my experience of you. I will sip
for all the waking day
the natural juices of your sweet tree
under which I lie, a new man
in an old idyll, always satisfied,
always hungry.

With what an excess of moderation
will I fail to surfeit myself, while I watch
my friends and rivals waking from bouts
of passion into the terrible
hangover of love.

I sit, and sip, and carve this
poem and hang it
in your branches.

Intrusion

We sat by a Scottish stream
in Massachusetts.
A groundhog observed us,
its whiskered face peering
from a hole in the ground
like a cartoon from World War I
and through the still, bright air
flew birds whose names
I did not know.

Suddenly, in front of us,
thirty yards away,
a twenty foot limb
crashed from an elm tree.

Now, three weeks later,
in a Scottish house in Scotland,
I tell myself
it was one of a million
dramatic acts
in the world of nature's
perpetually symbolic play
that, if we had not been there,
would have taken place anyway.

But it disturbs me. I try
to see it as no other than
the Scottish water crimpling away
through America and
the watchful face peering
from its dugout across
the No Man's Land that lies
between me and everything.

Proud Walkers

The gale, that was southwest when
given room to be
southwest in, pounced down on
Loch Sionascaig from any
direction, funnelled through
hill-gaps.

It raised curtains, Indian
ropetrick curtains of water
that moved in straight lines and
different directions. One wondered
what under-surface mechanism
slid these tall figures this way, that
way, crisscross ways
like ominous naked ladies
in a painting by Paul Delvaux.

If one bears down on your boat,
lean, lean to windward. That lady
is hard as a wall of water — one slap
and she'll have you foundered, as
ominous naked ladies are
apt to do.

Holy Moon

The moon burst in like a crowd
and the carpet and the dressingtable
became numinous — not in a holy way, quite,
though in a Middle Ages way, which is
a way of being holy.

I gazed at them, turned lacquer and
tapestry, and stole a look at my hands to see
if they had grown monastic. They
had.

The night outside filled
with the sounds of flagellation
and rapt singing — Raphael
did a quick job on the sky. Hooded figures
moved on no feet over rooftops.
I expected an ox.

But the moon goes, sideways.
The crowd withdrew.
My wafer-thin hands plumped
into the 20th century. And
the bottlestopper on the dressingtable
winked like a taper
and went out.

Painting — "The Blue Jar"

The blue jar jumps forward
thrust into the room
by the colours round about it.

I wonder,
since it's thrust forward,
what true thing lies
in the fictitious space
behind it.

I sink into my surroundings,
leaving in front of me a fictitious space
where I can be invented.

But the blue jar helplessly
presents itself. It holds out a truth
on a fiction. It keeps its place
by being out of it.

I admire the muscles of pigments
that can hold out a jar for years
without trembling.

Names

In that shallow water
swim extraordinary little fish
with extraordinary names
they don't know they've been given —
rock goby, lumpsucker, father lasher.

I sit among sea lavender and see it. Easy
to point and say buckthorn,
tamarisk, purple rocket.
But they no more know these names
than I know who named them.

I know your name and who named you.
But you have selves as secret from me
as blenny or butterfish.
I sit by you and see you
with eyes ignorant as a glasswort
and I name you and name you
and wonder how it is
that the weight of your name, the most ponderable
thing I know, should raise
my thoughts up
from one shallow pool to
another where
we move always sideways to each other, like
a velvet fiddler and a porcelain crab.

No Choice

I think about you
in as many ways as rain comes.

(I am growing, as I get older,
to hate metaphors — their exactness
and their inadequacy.)

Sometimes these thoughts are
a moistness, hardly falling, than which
nothing is more gentle:
sometimes, a rattling shower, a
bustling Spring-cleaning of the mind:
sometimes, a drowning downpour.

I am growing, as I get older,
to hate metaphor,
to love gentleness,
to fear downpours.